Digging into the Facts

A Biological Science Book on Fossils for Children

Children's Biological Science of Fossils Books

BOBO'S
LITTLE BRIANIAC BOOKS

educational & informative books for children
(PRE-K / K-12)

Discoveries of scientists, palaeontologist and archaeologists are awesome and fantastic!

These amazing discoveries help us know, among other things, howour planet looked millions of years ago.

Let's talk about the key resources that led to these discoveries—the fossils!

Learn about these records of past plants and animals, and be amazed at our Earth's amazing features!

Fossils and everything they give us...

The word fossils derives from the Latin word fossilis, meaning "dug up".

Fossils are the remains of living organisms belonging to a past geological age. The remains of organisms have remained buried in hardened mud, or even turned into minerals, for millions of years.

These are the traces or impressions of ancient plants and animals. When organisms die, their bodies are buried in the layers of sediment.

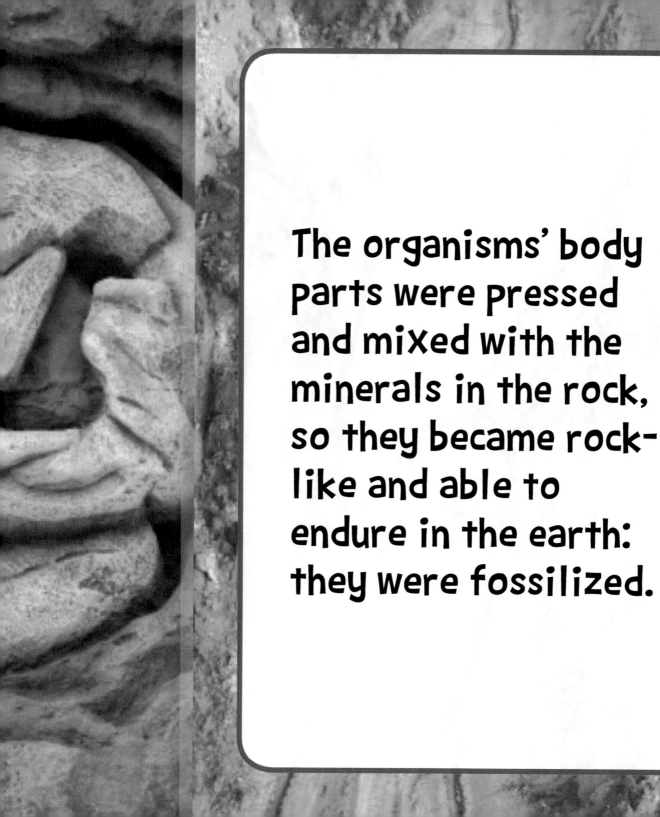

The organisms' body parts were pressed and mixed with the minerals in the rock, so they became rock-like and able to endure in the earth: they were fossilized.

For example, the fossil of a piece of bone didn't have the substance of a bone anymore. It may have the original shape of a bone but it's more of a rock.

It was chemically formed into a rock. So if you pick one up, expect it to be heavy like a rock. Most of the fossils ever discovered belong to extinct organisms.

What is the
branch of Science
that deals with
this study?

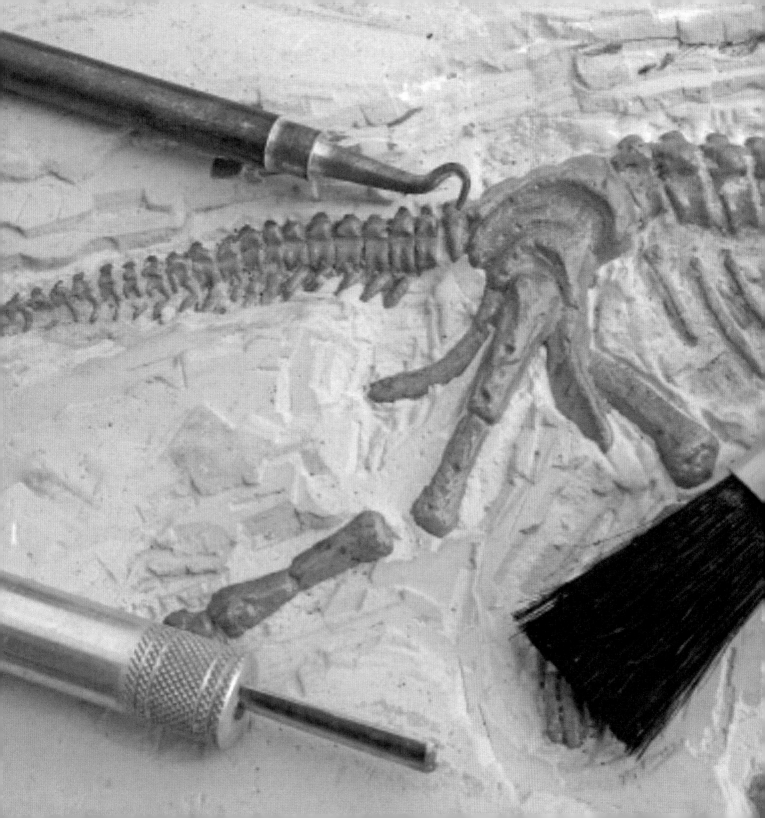

It is called Palaeontology. It is a branch of biology that primarily studies fossils to discover earlier forms of life in past geologic periods.

Through the discovered fossils, humankind learned about the existence of dinosaurs who lived long before humans came to be.

Fossils are found in any continents around the globe. Fossils can also be formed through "petrification".

In this process the hard and soft body parts of ancient organisms are replaced with organic materials and preserved.

These materials help in forming the ancient parts into rock-like fossils. The materials include calcite, pyrite and silica. Even wood can be petrified.

Insects and some plants have been preserved, compressed and embedded, in a hardened tree sap known as "amber".

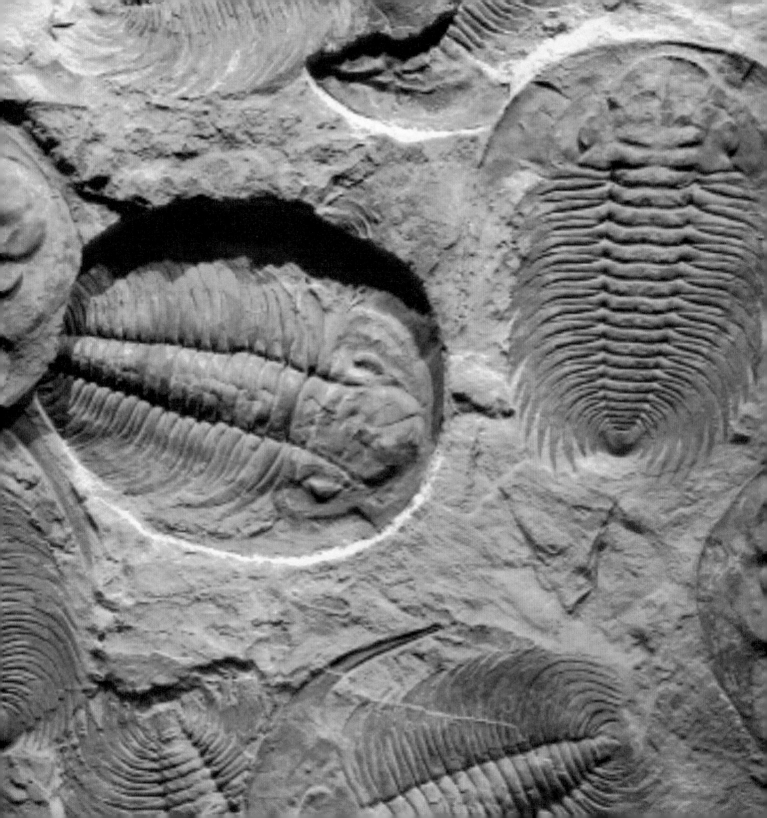

Insects were not turned into stones but they were completely intact within the tree resin that became amber.

Scientists found that dinosaur bones were petrified. But some geologic organism just decayed and did not fossilize.

As a result, there were no records left about their existence.

Palaeontologists estimate that the all the dinosaur species that we know through their fossilized remains are only a small percentage of all the types of dinosaur that once inhabited the planet.

But not all fossils come in the form of animal body parts. They might be footprints or even the burrows of ancient animals.

With fossilized footprints, scientists would be able to trace their historic routes of animals and even early people. This is a totally amazing gift fossils give us.

Not only that, scientists were able to discover fossilized poop of the dinosaur Tyrannosaurus Rex.

This poop is known as "coprolites". Scientists learned that the coprolites contained big pieces of crushed bones.

The blue-green algae in South Africa are the oldest fossils ever discovered. They lived on rocks 3.2 billion years ago.

It was in Thailand that the largest fossil was found. It was a petrified tree which was 72 meters long.

The amazing facts that the fossils brought to the world are being updated through ongoing studies.

To keep us informed about the enlightening facts, we have to keep track and read more about fossils.

Made in the USA
Middletown, DE
19 January 2023